Tao Te Ching

By

Lao Tzu

1

The Tao that can be trodden is not the
enduring and
unchanging Tao. The name that can be
named is not the enduring and
unchanging name.

(Conceived of as) having no name, it is
the Originator of heaven
and earth; (conceived of as) having a
name, it is the Mother of all
things.

Always without desire we must be
found,
If its deep mystery we would sound;
But if desire always within us be,
Its outer fringe is all that we shall see.

Under these two aspects, it is really the
same; but as development
takes place, it receives the different
names. Together we call them
the Mystery. Where the Mystery is the
deepest is the gate of all that
is subtle and wonderful.

2

All in the world know the beauty of the
beautiful, and in doing
this they have (the idea of) what
ugliness is; they all know the skill
of the skilful, and in doing this they
have (the idea of) what they
want of skill is.

So it is that existence and non-existence
give birth the one to
(the idea of) the other; that difficulty
and ease produce the one (the
idea of) the other; that length and
shortness fashion out the one the
figure of the other; that (the ideas of)
height and lowness arise from
the contrast of the one with the other;
that the musical notes and
tones become harmonious through the
relation of one with another; and
that being before and behind give the
idea of one following another.

Therefore the sage manages affairs
without doing anything, and

conveys his instructions without the use of speech.

All things spring up, and there is not
one which declines to show
itself; they grow, and there is no claim
made for their ownership;
they go through their processes, and
there is no expectation (of a
reward for the results). The work is
accomplished, and there is no
resting in it (as an achievement).

The work is done, but how no one can
see;
'Tis this that makes the power not cease
to be.

3

Not to value and employ men of
superior ability is the way to
keep the people from rivalry among
themselves; not to prize articles
which are difficult to procure is the
way to keep them from becoming

thieves; not to show them what is likely
to excite their desires is
the way to keep their minds from
disorder.

Therefore the sage, in the exercise of
his government, empties
their minds, fills their bellies, weakens
their wills, and strengthens
their bones.

He constantly (tries to) keep them
without knowledge and without
desire, and where there are those who
have knowledge, to keep them
from presuming to act (on it). When
there is this abstinence from
action, good order is universal.

4

The Tao is (like) the emptiness of a
vessel; and in our
employment of it we must be on our
guard against all fullness. How
deep and unfathomable it is, as if it

were the Honoured Ancestor of
all things!

We should blunt our sharp points, and
unravel the complications of
things; we should attemper our
brightness, and bring ourselves into
agreement with the obscurity of others.
How pure and still the Tao
is, as if it would ever so continue!

I do not know whose son it is. It might
appear to have been before
God.

5

Heaven and earth do not act from (the
impulse of) any wish to be
benevolent; they deal with all things as
the dogs of grass are dealt
with. The sages do not act from (any
wish to be) benevolent; they
deal with the people as the dogs of
grass are dealt with.

May not the space between heaven and
earth be compared to a
bellows?

'Tis emptied, yet it loses not its power;
'Tis moved again, and sends forth air
the more.
Much speech to swift exhaustion lead
we see;
Your inner being guard, and keep it
free.

6

The valley spirit dies not, aye the same;
The female mystery thus do we name.
Its gate, from which at first they issued
forth,
Is called the root from which grew
heaven and earth.
Long and unbroken does its power
remain,
Used gently, and without the touch of
pain.

7

Heaven is long-enduring and earth
continues long. The reason
why heaven and earth are able to
endure and continue thus long is
because they do not live of, or for,
themselves. This is how they are
able to continue and endure.

Therefore the sage puts his own person
last, and yet it is found in
the foremost place; he treats his person
as if it were foreign to him,
and yet that person is preserved. Is it
not because he has no
personal and private ends, that
therefore such ends are realised?

8

The highest excellence is like (that of)
water. The excellence
of water appears in its benefiting all
things, and in its occupying,
without striving (to the contrary), the

low place which all men
dislike. Hence (its way) is near to (that
of) the Tao.

The excellence of a residence is in (the
suitability of) the place;
that of the mind is in abysmal stillness;
that of associations is in
their being with the virtuous; that of
government is in its securing
good order; that of (the conduct of)
affairs is in its ability; and
that of (the initiation of) any movement
is in its timeliness.

And when (one with the highest
excellence) does not wrangle (about
his low position), no one finds fault
with him.

9

It is better to leave a vessel unfilled,
than to attempt to
carry it when it is full. If you keep
feeling a point that has been

sharpened, the point cannot long
preserve its sharpness.

When gold and jade fill the hall, their
possessor cannot keep them
safe. When wealth and honours lead to
arrogancy, this brings its evil
on itself. When the work is done, and
one's name is becoming
distinguished, to withdraw into
obscurity is the way of Heaven.

10

When the intelligent and animal souls
are held together in one
embrace, they can be kept from
separating. When one gives undivided
attention to the (vital) breathe, and
brings it to the utmost degree of
pliancy, he can become as a (tender)
babe. When he has cleansed away
the most mysterious sights (of his
imagination), he can become without
a flaw.

In loving the people and ruling the
state, cannot he proceed
without any (purpose of) action? In the
opening and shutting of his
gates of heaven, cannot he do so as a
female bird? While his
intelligence reaches in every direction,
cannot he (appear to) be
without knowledge?

(The Tao) produces (all things) and
nourishes them; it produces
them and does not claim them as its
own; it does all, and yet does not
boast of it; it presides over all, and yet
does not control them.
This is what is called 'The mysterious
Quality' (of the Tao).

11

The thirty spokes unite in the one nave;
but it is on the empty
space (for the axle), that the use of the
wheel depends. Clay is
fashioned into vessels; but it is on their

empty hollowness, that
their use depends. The door and
windows are cut out (from the walls)
to form an apartment; but it is on the
empty space (within), that its
use depends. Therefore, what has a
(positive) existence serves for
profitable adaptation, and what has not
that for (actual) usefulness.

12

Colour's five hues from th' eyes their
sight will take;
Music's five notes the ears as deaf can
make;
The flavours five deprive the mouth of
taste;
The chariot course, and the wild
hunting waste
Make mad the mind; and objects rare
and strange,
Sought for, men's conduct will to evil
change.

Therefore the sage seeks to satisfy (the

craving of) the belly, and
not the (insatiable longing of the) eyes.
He puts from him the
latter, and prefers to seek the former.

13

Favour and disgrace would seem
equally to be feared; honour and
great calamity, to be regarded as
personal conditions (of the same
kind).

What is meant by speaking thus of
favour and disgrace? Disgrace is
being in a low position (after the
enjoyment of favour). The getting
that (favour) leads to the apprehension
(of losing it), and the losing
it leads to the fear of (still greater
calamity):--this is what is
meant by saying that favour and
disgrace would seem equally to be
feared.

And what is meant by saying that

honour and great calamity are to be
(similarly) regarded as personal
conditions? What makes me liable to
great calamity is my having the body
(which I call myself); if I had
not the body, what great calamity could
come to me?

Therefore he who would administer the
kingdom, honouring it as he
honours his own person, may be
employed to govern it, and he who
would
administer it with the love which he
bears to his own person may be
entrusted with it.

14

We look at it, and we do not see it, and
we name it 'the
Equable.' We listen to it, and we do not
hear it, and we name it 'the
Inaudible.' We try to grasp it, and do
not get hold of it, and we
name it 'the Subtle.' With these three

qualities, it cannot be made
the subject of description; and hence
we blend them together and
obtain The One.

Its upper part is not bright, and its
lower part is not obscure.
Ceaseless in its action, it yet cannot be
named, and then it again
returns and becomes nothing. This is
called the Form of the Formless,
and the Semblance of the Invisible; this
is called the Fleeting and
Indeterminable.

We meet it and do not see its Front; we
follow it, and do not see
its Back. When we can lay hold of the
Tao of old to direct the things
of the present day, and are able to know
it as it was of old in the
beginning, this is called (unwinding)
the clue of Tao.

15

The skilful masters (of the Tao) in old
times, with a subtle
and exquisite penetration,
comprehended its mysteries, and were
deep
(also) so as to elude men's knowledge.
As they were thus beyond men's
knowledge, I will make an effort to
describe of what sort they
appeared to be.

Shrinking looked they like those who
wade through a stream in
winter; irresolute like those who are
afraid of all around them; grave
like a guest (in awe of his host);
evanescent like ice that is melting
away; unpretentious like wood that has
not been fashioned into
anything; vacant like a valley, and dull
like muddy water.

Who can (make) the muddy water
(clear)? Let it be still, and it
will gradually become clear. Who can

secure the condition of rest?
Let movement go on, and the condition
of rest will gradually arise.

They who preserve this method of the
Tao do not wish to be full (of
themselves). It is through their not
being full of themselves that
they can afford to seem worn and not
appear new and complete.

16

The (state of) vacancy should be
brought to the utmost degree,
and that of stillness guarded with
unwearying vigour. All things
alike go through their processes of
activity, and (then) we see them
return (to their original state). When
things (in the vegetable
world) have displayed their luxuriant
growth, we see each of them
return to its root. This returning to their
root is what we call the
state of stillness; and that stillness may

be called a reporting that
they have fulfilled their appointed end.

The report of that fulfilment is the
regular, unchanging rule. To
know that unchanging rule is to be
intelligent; not to know it leads
to wild movements and evil issues. The
knowledge of that unchanging
rule produces a (grand) capacity and
forbearance, and that capacity
and forbearance lead to a community
(of feeling with all things).
From this community of feeling comes
a kingliness of character; and he
who is king-like goes on to be heaven-
like. In that likeness to
heaven he possesses the Tao. Possessed
of the Tao, he endures long;
and to the end of his bodily life, is
exempt from all danger of decay.

17

In the highest antiquity, (the people)
did not know that there
were (their rulers). In the next age they
loved them and praised
them. In the next they feared them; in
the next they despised them.
Thus it was that when faith (in the Tao)
was deficient (in the rulers)
a want of faith in them ensued (in the
people).

How irresolute did those (earliest
rulers) appear, showing (by
their reticence) the importance which
they set upon their words!
Their work was done and their
undertakings were successful, while the
people all said, 'We are as we are, of
ourselves!'

18

When the Great Tao (Way or Method)
ceased to be observed,
benevolence and righteousness came
into vogue. (Then) appeared wisdom
and shrewdness, and there ensued great
hypocrisy.

When harmony no longer prevailed
throughout the six kinships,
filial sons found their manifestation;
when the states and clans fell
into disorder, loyal ministers appeared.

19

If we could renounce our sageness and
discard our wisdom, it
would be better for the people a
hundredfold. If we could renounce
our benevolence and discard our
righteousness, the people would again
become filial and kindly. If we could
renounce our artful
contrivances and discard our (scheming

for) gain, there would be no
thieves nor robbers.

Those three methods (of government)
Thought olden ways in elegance did
fail
And made these names their want of
worth to veil;
But simple views, and courses plain
and true
Would selfish ends and many lusts
eschew.

20

When we renounce learning we have
no troubles.
The (ready) 'yes,' and (flattering) 'yea;'-
-
Small is the difference they display.
But mark their issues, good and ill;--
What space the gulf between shall fill?

What all men fear is indeed to be
feared; but how wide and without end
is the range of questions (asking to be

discussed)!

The multitude of men look satisfied and
pleased; as if enjoying a
full banquet, as if mounted on a tower
in spring. I alone seem
listless and still, my desires having as
yet given no indication of
their presence. I am like an infant
which has not yet smiled. I look
dejected and forlorn, as if I had no
home to go to. The multitude of
men all have enough and to spare. I
alone seem to have lost
everything. My mind is that of a stupid
man; I am in a state of
chaos.

Ordinary men look bright and
intelligent, while I alone seem to be
benighted. They look full of
discrimination, while I alone am dull
and confused. I seem to be carried
about as on the sea, drifting as
if I had nowhere to rest. All men have
their spheres of action, while
I alone seem dull and incapable, like a

rude borderer. (Thus) I alone
am different from other men, but I
value the nursing-mother (the Tao).

21

The grandest forms of active force
From Tao come, their only source.
Who can of Tao the nature tell?
Our sight it flies, our touch as well.
Eluding sight, eluding touch,
The forms of things all in it crouch;
Eluding touch, eluding sight,
There are their semblances, all right.
Profound it is, dark and obscure;
Things' essences all there endure.
Those essences the truth enfold
Of what, when seen, shall then be told.
Now it is so; 'twas so of old.
Its name--what passes not away;
So, in their beautiful array,
Things form and never know decay.

How know I that it is so with all the
beauties of existing things? By
this (nature of the Tao).

22

The partial becomes complete; the
crooked, straight; the empty,
full; the worn out, new. He whose
(desires) are few gets them; he
whose (desires) are many goes astray.

Therefore the sage holds in his embrace
the one thing (of
humility), and manifests it to all the
world. He is free from self-
display, and therefore he shines; from
self-assertion, and therefore
he is distinguished; from self-boasting,
and therefore his merit is
acknowledged; from self-complacency,
and therefore he acquires
superiority. It is because he is thus free
from striving that
therefore no one in the world is able to
strive with him.

That saying of the ancients that 'the
partial becomes complete' was
not vainly spoken:--all real completion
is comprehended under it.

23

Abstaining from speech marks him
who is obeying the spontaneity
of his nature. A violent wind does not
last for a whole morning; a
sudden rain does not last for the whole
day. To whom is it that these
(two) things are owing? To Heaven and
Earth. If Heaven and Earth
cannot make such (spasmodic) actings
last long, how much less can man!

Therefore when one is making the Tao
his business, those who are
also pursuing it, agree with him in it,
and those who are making the
manifestation of its course their object
agree with him in that; while
even those who are failing in both these
things agree with him where
they fail.

Hence, those with whom he agrees as
to the Tao have the happiness
of attaining to it; those with whom he
agrees as to its manifestation

have the happiness of attaining to it;
and those with whom he agrees
in their failure have also the happiness
of attaining (to the Tao).
(But) when there is not faith sufficient
(on his part), a want of
faith (in him) ensues (on the part of the
others).

24

He who stands on his tiptoes does not
stand firm; he who stretches
his legs does not walk (easily). (So), he
who displays himself does
not shine; he who asserts his own views
is not distinguished; he who
vaunts himself does not find his merit
acknowledged; he who is self-
conceited has no superiority allowed to
him. Such conditions, viewed
from the standpoint of the Tao, are like
remnants of food, or a tumour
on the body, which all dislike. Hence
those who pursue (the course)

of the Tao do not adopt and allow
them.

25

There was something undefined and
complete, coming into
existence before Heaven and Earth.
How still it was and formless,
standing alone, and undergoing no
change, reaching everywhere and in
no danger (of being exhausted)! It may
be regarded as the Mother of
all things.

I do not know its name, and I give it the
designation of the Tao
(the Way or Course). Making an effort
(further) to give it a name I
call it The Great.

Great, it passes on (in constant flow).
Passing on, it becomes
remote. Having become remote, it
returns. Therefore the Tao is
great; Heaven is great; Earth is great;
and the (sage) king is also

great. In the universe there are four that
are great, and the (sage)
king is one of them.

Man takes his law from the Earth; the
Earth takes its law from
Heaven; Heaven takes its law from the
Tao. The law of the Tao is its
being what it is.

26

Gravity is the root of lightness;
stillness, the ruler of
movement.

Therefore a wise prince, marching the
whole day, does not go far
from his baggage waggons. Although
he may have brilliant prospects to
look at, he quietly remains (in his
proper place), indifferent to
them. How should the lord of a myriad
chariots carry himself lightly
before the kingdom? If he do act
lightly, he has lost his root (of

gravity); if he proceed to active movement, he will lose his throne.

27

The skilful traveller leaves no traces of his wheels or
footsteps; the skilful speaker says nothing that can be found fault
with or blamed; the skilful reckoner uses no tallies; the skilful
closer needs no bolts or bars, while to open what he has shut will be
impossible; the skilful binder uses no strings or knots, while to
unloose what he has bound will be impossible. In the same way the
sage is always skilful at saving men, and so he does not cast away any
man; he is always skilful at saving things, and so he does not cast
away anything. This is called 'Hiding the light of his procedure.'

Therefore the man of skill is a master (to be looked up to) by him

who has not the skill; and he who has
not the skill is the helper of
(the reputation of) him who has the
skill. If the one did not honour
his master, and the other did not rejoice
in his helper, an
(observer), though intelligent, might
greatly err about them. This is
called 'The utmost degree of mystery.'

28

Who knows his manhood's strength,
Yet still his female feebleness
maintains;
As to one channel flow the many
drains,
All come to him, yea, all beneath the
sky.
Thus he the constant excellence retains;
The simple child again, free from all
stains.

Who knows how white attracts,
Yet always keeps himself within
black's shade,

The pattern of humility displayed,
Displayed in view of all beneath the
sky;
He in the unchanging excellence
arrayed,
Endless return to man's first state has
made.

Who knows how glory shines,
Yet loves disgrace, nor e'er for it is
pale;
Behold his presence in a spacious vale,
To which men come from all beneath
the sky.
The unchanging excellence completes
its tale;
The simple infant man in him we hail.

The unwrought material, when divided
and distributed, forms
vessels. The sage, when employed,
becomes the Head of all the
Officers (of government); and in his
greatest regulations he employs
no violent measures.

29

If any one should wish to get the
kingdom for himself, and to
effect this by what he does, I see that he
will not succeed. The
kingdom is a spirit-like thing, and
cannot be got by active doing. He
who would so win it destroys it; he who
would hold it in his grasp
loses it.

The course and nature of things is such
that
What was in front is now behind;
What warmed anon we freezing find.
Strength is of weakness oft the spoil;
The store in ruins mocks our toil.

Hence the sage puts away excessive
effort, extravagance, and easy
indulgence.

30

He who would assist a lord of men in
harmony with the Tao will
not assert his mastery in the kingdom
by force of arms. Such a course
is sure to meet with its proper return.

Wherever a host is stationed, briars and
thorns spring up. In the
sequence of great armies there are sure
to be bad years.

A skilful (commander) strikes a
decisive blow, and stops. He does
not dare (by continuing his operations)
to assert and complete his
mastery. He will strike the blow, but
will be on his guard against
being vain or boastful or arrogant in
consequence of it. He strikes
it as a matter of necessity; he strikes it,
but not from a wish for
mastery.

When things have attained their strong
maturity they become old.

This may be said to be not in
accordance with the Tao: and what is
not
in accordance with it soon comes to an
end.

31

Now arms, however beautiful, are
instruments of evil omen,
hateful, it may be said, to all creatures.
Therefore they who have
the Tao do not like to employ them.

The superior man ordinarily considers
the left hand the most
honourable place, but in time of war the
right hand. Those sharp
weapons are instruments of evil omen,
and not the instruments of the
superior man;--he uses them only on
the compulsion of necessity. Calm
and repose are what he prizes; victory
(by force of arms) is to him
undesirable. To consider this desirable
would be to delight in the

slaughter of men; and he who delights
in the slaughter of men cannot
get his will in the kingdom.

On occasions of festivity to be on the
left hand is the prized
position; on occasions of mourning, the
right hand. The second in
command of the army has his place on
the left; the general commanding
in chief has his on the right;--his place,
that is, is assigned to him
as in the rites of mourning. He who has
killed multitudes of men
should weep for them with the bitterest
grief; and the victor in
battle has his place (rightly) according
to those rites.

32

The Tao, considered as unchanging,
has no name.

Though in its primordial simplicity it
may be small, the whole

world dares not deal with (one embodying) it as a minister. If a feudal prince or the king could guard and hold it, all would spontaneously submit themselves to him.

Heaven and Earth (under its guidance) unite together and send down the sweet dew, which, without the directions of men, reaches equally everywhere as of its own accord.

As soon as it proceeds to action, it has a name. When it once has that name, (men) can know to rest in it. When they know to rest in it, they can be free from all risk of failure and error.

The relation of the Tao to all the world is like that of the great rivers and seas to the streams from the valleys.

33

He who knows other men is discerning;
he who knows himself is
intelligent. He who overcomes others is
strong; he who overcomes
himself is mighty. He who is satisfied
with his lot is rich; he who
goes on acting with energy has a (firm)
will.

He who does not fail in the
requirements of his position, continues
long; he who dies and yet does not
perish, has longevity.

34

All-pervading is the Great Tao! It may
be found on the left
hand and on the right.

All things depend on it for their
production, which it gives to
them, not one refusing obedience to it.
When its work is

accomplished, it does not claim the name of having done it. It clothes all things as with a garment, and makes no assumption of being their lord;--it may be named in the smallest things. All things return (to their root and disappear), and do not know that it is it which presides over their doing so;--it may be named in the greatest things.

Hence the sage is able (in the same way) to accomplish his great achievements. It is through his not making himself great that he can accomplish them.

35

To him who holds in his hands the Great Image (of the invisible Tao), the whole world repairs. Men resort to him, and receive no hurt, but (find) rest, peace, and the feeling of ease.

Music and dainties will make the
passing guest stop (for a time).
But though the Tao as it comes from
the mouth, seems insipid and has
no flavour, though it seems not worth
being looked at or listened to,
the use of it is inexhaustible.

36

When one is about to take an
inspiration, he is sure to make a
(previous) expiration; when he is going
to weaken another, he will
first strengthen him; when he is going
to overthrow another, he will
first have raised him up; when he is
going to despoil another, he will
first have made gifts to him:--this is
called 'Hiding the light (of
his procedure).'

The soft overcomes the hard; and the
weak the strong.

Fishes should not be taken from the
deep; instruments for the
profit of a state should not be shown to
the people.

37

The Tao in its regular course does
nothing (for the sake of
doing it), and so there is nothing which
it does not do.

If princes and kings were able to
maintain it, all things would of
themselves be transformed by them.

If this transformation became to me an
object of desire, I would
express the desire by the nameless
simplicity.

Simplicity without a name
Is free from all external aim.
With no desire, at rest and still,
All things go right as of their will.

38

(Those who) possessed in highest
degree the attributes (of the
Tao) did not (seek) to show them, and
therefore they possessed them
(in fullest measure). (Those who)
possessed in a lower degree those
attributes (sought how) not to lose
them, and therefore they did not
possess them (in fullest measure).

(Those who) possessed in the highest
degree those attributes did
nothing (with a purpose), and had no
need to do anything. (Those who)
possessed them in a lower degree were
(always) doing, and had need to
be so doing.

(Those who) possessed the highest
benevolence were (always seeking)
to carry it out, and had no need to be
doing so. (Those who)
possessed the highest righteousness
were (always seeking) to carry it
out, and had need to be so doing.

(Those who) possessed the highest
(sense of) propriety were (always
seeking) to show it, and when men did
not respond to it, they bared
the arm and marched up to them.

Thus it was that when the Tao was lost,
its attributes appeared;
when its attributes were lost,
benevolence appeared; when
benevolence
was lost, righteousness appeared; and
when righteousness was lost, the
proprieties appeared.

Now propriety is the attenuated form of
leal-heartedness and good
faith, and is also the commencement of
disorder; swift apprehension is
(only) a flower of the Tao, and is the
beginning of stupidity.

Thus it is that the Great man abides by
what is solid, and eschews
what is flimsy; dwells with the fruit and
not with the flower. It is

thus that he puts away the one and
makes choice of the other.

39

The things which from of old have got
the One (the Tao) are--

Heaven which by it is bright and pure;
Earth rendered thereby firm and sure;
Spirits with powers by it supplied;
Valleys kept full throughout their void
All creatures which through it do live
Princes and kings who from it get
The model which to all they give.

All these are the results of the One
(Tao).

If heaven were not thus pure, it soon
would rend;
If earth were not thus sure, 'twould
break and bend;
Without these powers, the spirits soon
would fail;
If not so filled, the drought would parch

each vale;
Without that life, creatures would pass
away;
Princes and kings, without that moral
sway,
However grand and high, would all
decay.

Thus it is that dignity finds its (firm)
root in its (previous)
meanness, and what is lofty finds its
stability in the lowness (from
which it rises). Hence princes and kings
call themselves 'Orphans,'
'Men of small virtue,' and as 'Carriages
without a nave.' Is not this
an acknowledgment that in their
considering themselves mean they see
the foundation of their dignity? So it is
that in the enumeration of
the different parts of a carriage we do
not come on what makes it
answer the ends of a carriage. They do
not wish to show themselves
elegant-looking as jade, but (prefer) to
be coarse-looking as an
(ordinary) stone.

40

The movement of the Tao
By contraries proceeds;
And weakness marks the course
Of Tao's mighty deeds.

All things under heaven sprang from It
as existing (and named);
that existence sprang from It as non-
existent (and not named).

41

Scholars of the highest class, when they
hear about the Tao,
earnestly carry it into practice. Scholars
of the middle class, when
they have heard about it, seem now to
keep it and now to lose it.
Scholars of the lowest class, when they
have heard about it, laugh
greatly at it. If it were not (thus)
laughed at, it would not be fit
to be the Tao.

Therefore the sentence-makers have thus expressed themselves:--

'The Tao, when brightest seen, seems light to lack;
Who progress in it makes, seems drawing back;
Its even way is like a rugged track.
Its highest virtue from the vale doth rise;
Its greatest beauty seems to offend the eyes;
And he has most whose lot the least supplies.
Its firmest virtue seems but poor and low;
Its solid truth seems change to undergo;
Its largest square doth yet no corner show
A vessel great, it is the slowest made;
Loud is its sound, but never word it said;
A semblance great, the shadow of a shade.'

The Tao is hidden, and has no name; but it is the Tao which is

skilful at imparting (to all things what
they need) and making them
complete.

42

The Tao produced One; One produced
Two; Two produced Three;
Three produced All things. All things
leave behind them the Obscurity
(out of which they have come), and go
forward to embrace the
Brightness (into which they have
emerged), while they are harmonised
by the Breath of Vacancy.

What men dislike is to be orphans, to
have little virtue, to be as
carriages without naves; and yet these
are the designations which
kings and princes use for themselves.
So it is that some things are
increased by being diminished, and
others are diminished by being
increased.

What other men (thus) teach, I also
teach. The violent and strong
do not die their natural death. I will
make this the basis of my
teaching.

43

The softest thing in the world dashes
against and overcomes the
hardest; that which has no (substantial)
existence enters where there
is no crevice. I know hereby what
advantage belongs to doing nothing
(with a purpose).

There are few in the world who attain
to the teaching without
words, and the advantage arising from
non-action.

44

Or fame or life,
Which do you hold more dear?
Or life or wealth,
To which would you adhere?
Keep life and lose those other things;
Keep them and lose your life:--which
brings
Sorrow and pain more near?

Thus we may see,
Who cleaves to fame
Rejects what is more great;
Who loves large stores
Gives up the richer state.

Who is content
Needs fear no shame.
Who knows to stop
Incurs no blame.
From danger free
Long live shall he.

45

Who thinks his great achievements
poor
Shall find his vigour long endure.
Of greatest fulness, deemed a void,
Exhaustion ne'er shall stem the tide.
Do thou what's straight still crooked
deem;
Thy greatest art still stupid seem,
And eloquence a stammering scream.

Constant action overcomes cold; being
still overcomes heat. Purity
and stillness give the correct law to all
under heaven.

46

When the Tao prevails in the world,
they send back their swift
horses to (draw) the dung-carts. When
the Tao is disregarded in the
world, the war-horses breed in the
border lands.

There is no guilt greater than to
sanction ambition; no calamity
greater than to be discontented with
one's lot; no fault greater than
the wish to be getting. Therefore the
sufficiency of contentment is
an enduring and unchanging
sufficiency.

47

Without going outside his door, one
understands (all that takes
place) under the sky; without looking
out from his window, one sees
the Tao of Heaven. The farther that one
goes out (from himself), the
less he knows.

Therefore the sages got their
knowledge without travelling; gave
their (right) names to things without
seeing them; and accomplished
their ends without any purpose of doing
so.

48

He who devotes himself to learning
(seeks) from day to day to
increase (his knowledge); he who
devotes himself to the Tao (seeks)
from day to day to diminish (his doing).

He diminishes it and again diminishes
it, till he arrives at doing
nothing (on purpose). Having arrived at
this point of non-action,
there is nothing which he does not do.

He who gets as his own all under
heaven does so by giving himself
no trouble (with that end). If one take
trouble (with that end), he
is not equal to getting as his own all
under heaven.

49

The sage has no invariable mind of his
own; he makes the mind
of the people his mind.

To those who are good (to me), I am
good; and to those who are not
good (to me), I am also good;--and thus
(all) get to be good. To
those who are sincere (with me), I am
sincere; and to those who are
not sincere (with me), I am also
sincere;--and thus (all) get to be
sincere.

The sage has in the world an
appearance of indecision, and keeps
his mind in a state of indifference to all.
The people all keep their
eyes and ears directed to him, and he
deals with them all as his
children.

50

Men come forth and live; they enter
(again) and die.

Of every ten three are ministers of life
(to themselves); and three
are ministers of death.

There are also three in every ten whose aim is to live, but whose movements tend to the land (or place) of death. And for what reason? Because of their excessive endeavours to perpetuate life.

But I have heard that he who is skilful in managing the life entrusted to him for a time travels on the land without having to shun rhinoceros or tiger, and enters a host without having to avoid buff coat or sharp weapon. The rhinoceros finds no place in him into which to thrust its horn, nor the tiger a place in which to fix its claws, nor the weapon a place to admit its point. And for what reason? Because there is in him no place of death.

51

All things are produced by the Tao, and
nourished by its
outflowing operation. They receive
their forms according to the
nature of each, and are completed
according to the circumstances of
their condition. Therefore all things
without exception honour the
Tao, and exalt its outflowing operation.

This honouring of the Tao and exalting
of its operation is not the
result of any ordination, but always a
spontaneous tribute.

Thus it is that the Tao produces (all
things), nourishes them,
brings them to their full growth, nurses
them, completes them, matures
them, maintains them, and overspreads
them.

It produces them and makes no claim to
the possession of them; it
carries them through their processes

and does not vaunt its ability in
doing so; it brings them to maturity and
exercises no control over
them;--this is called its mysterious
operation.

52

(The Tao) which originated all under
the sky is to be
considered as the mother of them all.

When the mother is found, we know
what her children should be.
When one knows that he is his mother's
child, and proceeds to guard
(the qualities of) the mother that belong
to him, to the end of his
life he will be free from all peril.

Let him keep his mouth closed, and
shut up the portals (of his
nostrils), and all his life he will be
exempt from laborious exertion.
Let him keep his mouth open, and
(spend his breath) in the promotion

of his affairs, and all his life there will
be no safety for him.

The perception of what is small is (the
secret of clear-
sightedness; the guarding of what is
soft and tender is (the secret
of) strength.

Who uses well his light,
Reverting to its (source so) bright,
Will from his body ward all blight,
And hides the unchanging from men's
sight.

53

If I were suddenly to become known,
and (put into a position
to) conduct (a government) according
to the Great Tao, what I should
be most afraid of would be a boastful
display.

The great Tao (or way) is very level
and easy; but people love the

by-ways.

Their court(-yards and buildings) shall
be well kept, but their
fields shall be ill-cultivated, and their
granaries very empty. They
shall wear elegant and ornamented
robes, carry a sharp sword at their
girdle, pamper themselves in eating and
drinking, and have a
superabundance of property and
wealth;--such (princes) may be called
robbers and boasters. This is contrary
to the Tao surely!

54

What (Tao's) skilful planter plants
Can never be uptorn;
What his skilful arms enfold,
From him can ne'er be borne.
Sons shall bring in lengthening line,
Sacrifices to his shrine.

Tao when nursed within one's self,
His vigour will make true;

And where the family it rules
What riches will accrue!
The neighbourhood where it prevails
In thriving will abound;
And when 'tis seen throughout the state,
Good fortune will be found.
Employ it the kingdom o'er,
And men thrive all around.

In this way the effect will be seen in the person, by the
observation of different cases; in the
family; in the neighbourhood;
in the state; and in the kingdom.

How do I know that this effect is sure
to hold thus all under the
sky? By this (method of observation).

55

He who has in himself abundantly the
attributes (of the Tao) is
like an infant. Poisonous insects will
not sting him; fierce beasts
will not seize him; birds of prey will

not strike him.

(The infant's) bones are weak and its
sinews soft, but yet its
grasp is firm. It knows not yet the
union of male and female, and yet
its virile member may be excited;--
showing the perfection of its
physical essence. All day long it will
cry without its throat
becoming hoarse;--showing the
harmony (in its constitution).

To him by whom this harmony is
known,
(The secret of) the unchanging (Tao) is
shown,
And in the knowledge wisdom finds its
throne.
All life-increasing arts to evil turn;
Where the mind makes the vital breath
to burn,
(False) is the strength, (and o'er it we
should mourn.)

When things have become strong, they
(then) become old, which may

be said to be contrary to the Tao.
Whatever is contrary to the Tao
soon ends.

56

He who knows (the Tao) does not (care
to) speak (about it); he
who is (ever ready to) speak about it
does not know it.

He (who knows it) will keep his mouth
shut and close the portals
(of his nostrils). He will blunt his sharp
points and unravel the
complications of things; he will
attemper his brightness, and bring
himself into agreement with the
obscurity (of others). This is called
'the Mysterious Agreement.'

(Such an one) cannot be treated
familiarly or distantly; he is
beyond all consideration of profit or
injury; of nobility or

meanness:--he is the noblest man under
heaven.

57

A state may be ruled by (measures of)
correction; weapons of
war may be used with crafty dexterity;
(but) the kingdom is made one's
own (only) by freedom from action and
purpose.

How do I know that it is so? By these
facts:--In the kingdom the
multiplication of prohibitive
enactments increases the poverty of the
people; the more implements to add to
their profit that the people
have, the greater disorder is there in the
state and clan; the more
acts of crafty dexterity that men
possess, the more do strange
contrivances appear; the more display
there is of legislation, the
more thieves and robbers there are.

Therefore a sage has said, 'I will do
nothing (of purpose), and the
people will be transformed of
themselves; I will be fond of keeping
still, and the people will of themselves
become correct. I will take
no trouble about it, and the people will
of themselves become rich; I
will manifest no ambition, and the
people will of themselves attain to
the primitive simplicity.'

58

The government that seems the most
unwise,
Oft goodness to the people best
supplies;
That which is meddling, touching
everything,
Will work but ill, and disappointment
bring.

Misery!--happiness is to be found by its
side! Happiness!--misery
lurks beneath it! Who knows what

either will come to in the end?

Shall we then dispense with correction?
The (method of) correction
shall by a turn become distortion, and
the good in it shall by a turn
become evil. The delusion of the
people (on this point) has indeed
subsisted for a long time.

Therefore the sage is (like) a square
which cuts no one (with its
angles); (like) a corner which injures no
one (with its sharpness).
He is straightforward, but allows
himself no license; he is bright,
but does not dazzle.

59

For regulating the human (in our
constitution) and rendering
the (proper) service to the heavenly,
there is nothing like
moderation.

It is only by this moderation that there is effected an early
return (to man's normal state). That early return is what I call the
repeated accumulation of the attributes (of the Tao). With that
repeated accumulation of those attributes, there comes the subjugation
(of every obstacle to such return). Of this subjugation we know not
what shall be the limit; and when one knows not what the limit shall
be, he may be the ruler of a state.

He who possesses the mother of the state may continue long. His
case is like that (of the plant) of which we say that its roots are
deep and its flower stalks firm:--this is the way to secure that its
enduring life shall long be seen.

60

Governing a great state is like cooking
small fish.

Let the kingdom be governed according
to the Tao, and the manes of
the departed will not manifest their
spiritual energy. It is not that
those manes have not that spiritual
energy, but it will not be
employed to hurt men. It is not that it
could not hurt men, but
neither does the ruling sage hurt them.

When these two do not injuriously
affect each other, their good
influences converge in the virtue (of the
Tao).

61

What makes a great state is its being
(like) a low-lying, down-
flowing (stream);--it becomes the
centre to which tend (all the small

states) under heaven.

(To illustrate from) the case of all
females:--the female always
overcomes the male by her stillness.
Stillness may be considered (a
sort of) abasement.

Thus it is that a great state, by
condescending to small states,
gains them for itself; and that small
states, by abasing themselves to
a great state, win it over to them. In the
one case the abasement
leads to gaining adherents, in the other
case to procuring favour.

The great state only wishes to unite
men together and nourish them;
a small state only wishes to be received
by, and to serve, the other.
Each gets what it desires, but the great
state must learn to abase
itself.

62

Tao has of all things the most honoured
place.
No treasures give good men so rich a
grace;
Bad men it guards, and doth their ill
efface.

(Its) admirable words can purchase
honour; (its) admirable deeds
can raise their performer above others.
Even men who are not good are
not abandoned by it.

Therefore when the sovereign occupies
his place as the Son of
Heaven, and he has appointed his three
ducal ministers, though (a
prince) were to send in a round symbol-
of-rank large enough to fill
both the hands, and that as the
precursor of the team of horses (in
the court-yard), such an offering would
not be equal to (a lesson of)
this Tao, which one might present on
his knees.

Why was it that the ancients prized this
Tao so much? Was it not
because it could be got by seeking for
it, and the guilty could escape
(from the stain of their guilt) by it? This
is the reason why all
under heaven consider it the most
valuable thing.

63

(It is the way of the Tao) to act without
(thinking of) acting;
to conduct affairs without (feeling the)
trouble of them; to taste
without discerning any flavour; to
consider what is small as great,
and a few as many; and to recompense
injury with kindness.

(The master of it) anticipates things that
are difficult while they
are easy, and does things that would
become great while they are
small. All difficult things in the world

are sure to arise from a
previous state in which they were easy,
and all great things from one
in which they were small. Therefore the
sage, while he never does
what is great, is able on that account to
accomplish the greatest
things.

He who lightly promises is sure to keep
but little faith; he who is
continually thinking things easy is sure
to find them difficult.
Therefore the sage sees difficulty even
in what seems easy, and so
never has any difficulties.

64

That which is at rest is easily kept hold
of; before a thing
has given indications of its presence, it
is easy to take measures
against it; that which is brittle is easily
broken; that which is very
small is easily dispersed. Action should

be taken before a thing has
made its appearance; order should be
secured before disorder has
begun.

The tree which fills the arms grew from
the tiniest sprout; the
tower of nine storeys rose from a
(small) heap of earth; the journey
of a thousand li commenced with a
single step.

He who acts (with an ulterior purpose)
does harm; he who takes hold
of a thing (in the same way) loses his
hold. The sage does not act
(so), and therefore does no harm; he
does not lay hold (so), and
therefore does not lose his bold. (But)
people in their conduct of
affairs are constantly ruining them
when they are on the eve of
success. If they were careful at the end,
as (they should be) at the
beginning, they would not so ruin them.

Therefore the sage desires what (other

men) do not desire, and does
not prize things difficult to get; he
learns what (other men) do not
learn, and turns back to what the
multitude of men have passed by.
Thus he helps the natural development
of all things, and does not dare
to act (with an ulterior purpose of his
own).

65

The ancients who showed their skill in
practising the Tao did
so, not to enlighten the people, but
rather to make them simple and
ignorant.

The difficulty in governing the people
arises from their having
much knowledge. He who (tries to)
govern a state by his wisdom is a
scourge to it; while he who does not
(try to) do so is a blessing.

He who knows these two things finds

in them also his model and
rule. Ability to know this model and
rule constitutes what we call
the mysterious excellence (of a
governor). Deep and far-reaching is
such mysterious excellence, showing
indeed its possessor as opposite
to others, but leading them to a great
conformity to him.

66

That whereby the rivers and seas are
able to receive the homage
and tribute of all the valley streams, is
their skill in being lower
than they;--it is thus that they are the
kings of them all. So it is
that the sage (ruler), wishing to be
above men, puts himself by his
words below them, and, wishing to be
before them, places his person
behind them.

In this way though he has his place
above them, men do not feel his

weight, nor though he has his place
before them, do they feel it an
injury to them.

Therefore all in the world delight to
exalt him and do not weary of
him. Because he does not strive, no one
finds it possible to strive
with him.

67

All the world says that, while my Tao
is great, it yet appears
to be inferior (to other systems of
teaching). Now it is just its
greatness that makes it seem to be
inferior. If it were like any
other (system), for long would its
smallness have been known!

But I have three precious things which
I prize and hold fast. The
first is gentleness; the second is
economy; and the third is shrinking
from taking precedence of others.

With that gentleness I can be bold; with
that economy I can be
liberal; shrinking from taking
precedence of others, I can become a
vessel of the highest honour. Now-a-
days they give up gentleness and
are all for being bold; economy, and are
all for being liberal; the
hindmost place, and seek only to be
foremost;--(of all which the end
is) death.

Gentleness is sure to be victorious even
in battle, and firmly to
maintain its ground. Heaven will save
its possessor, by his (very)
gentleness protecting him.

68

He who in (Tao's) wars has skill
Assumes no martial port;
He who fights with most good will
To rage makes no resort.
He who vanquishes yet still
Keeps from his foes apart;

He whose hests men most fulfil
Yet humbly plies his art.

Thus we say, 'He ne'er contends,
And therein is his might.'
Thus we say, 'Men's wills he bends,
That they with him unite.'
Thus we say, 'Like Heaven's his ends,
No sage of old more bright.'

69

A master of the art of war has said, 'I
do not dare to be the
host (to commence the war); I prefer to
be the guest (to act on the
defensive). I do not dare to advance an
inch; I prefer to retire a
foot.' This is called marshalling the
ranks where there are no ranks;
baring the arms (to fight) where there
are no arms to bare; grasping
the weapon where there is no weapon
to grasp; advancing against the
enemy where there is no enemy.

There is no calamity greater than
lightly engaging in war. To do
that is near losing (the gentleness)
which is so precious. Thus it is
that when opposing weapons are
(actually) crossed, he who deplores
(the situation) conquers.

70

My words are very easy to know, and
very easy to practise; but
there is no one in the world who is able
to know and able to practise
them.

There is an originating and all-
comprehending (principle) in my
words, and an authoritative law for the
things (which I enforce). It
is because they do not know these, that
men do not know me.

They who know me are few, and I am
on that account (the more) to be
prized. It is thus that the sage wears (a

poor garb of) hair cloth,
while he carries his (signet of) jade in
his bosom.

71

To know and yet (think) we do not
know is the highest
(attainment); not to know (and yet
think) we do know is a disease.

It is simply by being pained at (the
thought of) having this
disease that we are preserved from it.
The sage has not the disease.
He knows the pain that would be
inseparable from it, and therefore he
does not have it.

72

When the people do not fear what they
ought to fear, that which
is their great dread will come on them.

Let them not thoughtlessly indulge
themselves in their ordinary
life; let them not act as if weary of what
that life depends on.

It is by avoiding such indulgence that
such weariness does not
arise.

Therefore the sage knows (these things)
of himself, but does not
parade (his knowledge); loves, but does
not (appear to set a) value
on, himself. And thus he puts the latter
alternative away and makes
choice of the former.

73

He whose boldness appears in his
daring (to do wrong, in
defiance of the laws) is put to death; he
whose boldness appears in
his not daring (to do so) lives on. Of
these two cases the one
appears to be advantageous, and the

other to be injurious. But

When Heaven's anger smites a man,
Who the cause shall truly scan?

On this account the sage feels a
difficulty (as to what to do in the
former case).

It is the way of Heaven not to strive,
and yet it skilfully
overcomes; not to speak, and yet it is
skilful in (obtaining a reply;
does not call, and yet men come to it of
themselves. Its
demonstrations are quiet, and yet its
plans are skilful and effective.
The meshes of the net of Heaven are
large; far apart, but letting
nothing escape.

74

The people do not fear death; to what
purpose is it to (try to)
frighten them with death? If the people

were always in awe of death,
and I could always seize those who do
wrong, and put them to death,
who would dare to do wrong?

There is always One who presides over
the infliction death. He who
would inflict death in the room of him
who so presides over it may be
described as hewing wood instead of a
great carpenter. Seldom is it
that he who undertakes the hewing,
instead of the great carpenter,
does not cut his own hands!

75

The people suffer from famine because
of the multitude of taxes
consumed by their superiors. It is
through this that they suffer
famine.

The people are difficult to govern
because of the (excessive)
agency of their superiors (in governing
them). It is through this

that they are difficult to govern.

The people make light of dying because
of the greatness of their
labours in seeking for the means of
living. It is this which makes
them think light of dying. Thus it is that
to leave the subject of
living altogether out of view is better
than to set a high value on
it.

76

Man at his birth is supple and weak; at
his death, firm and
strong. (So it is with) all things. Trees
and plants, in their early
growth, are soft and brittle; at their
death, dry and withered.

Thus it is that firmness and strength are
the concomitants of
death; softness and weakness, the
concomitants of life.

Hence he who (relies on) the strength
of his forces does not
conquer; and a tree which is strong will
fill the out-stretched arms,
(and thereby invites the feller.)

Therefore the place of what is firm and
strong is below, and that
of what is soft and weak is above.

77

May not the Way (or Tao) of Heaven
be compared to the (method

of) bending a bow? The (part of the
bow) which was high is brought
low, and what was low is raised up. (So
Heaven) diminishes where
there is superabundance, and
supplements where there is deficiency.

It is the Way of Heaven to diminish
superabundance, and to
supplement deficiency. It is not so with
the way of man. He takes

away from those who have not enough
to add to his own superabundance.

Who can take his own superabundance
and therewith serve all under
heaven? Only he who is in possession
of the Tao!

Therefore the (ruling) sage acts without
claiming the results as
his; he achieves his merit and does not
rest (arrogantly) in it:--he
does not wish to display his superiority.

78

There is nothing in the world more soft
and weak than water,
and yet for attacking things that are
firm and strong there is nothing
that can take precedence of it;--for
there is nothing (so effectual)
for which it can be changed.

Every one in the world knows that the
soft overcomes the hard, and

the weak the strong, but no one is able
to carry it out in practice.

Therefore a sage has said,
'He who accepts his state's reproach,
Is hailed therefore its altars' lord;
To him who bears men's direful woes
They all the name of King accord.'

Words that are strictly true seem to be
paradoxical.

79

When a reconciliation is effected
(between two parties) after a
great animosity, there is sure to be a
grudge remaining (in the mind
of the one who was wrong). And how
can this be beneficial (to the
other)?

Therefore (to guard against this), the
sage keeps the left-hand
portion of the record of the
engagement, and does not insist on the

(speedy) fulfilment of it by the other
party. (So), he who has the
attributes (of the Tao) regards (only)
the conditions of the
engagement, while he who has not
those attributes regards only the
conditions favourable to himself.

In the Way of Heaven, there is no
partiality of love; it is always
on the side of the good man.

80

In a little state with a small population,
I would so order it,
that, though there were individuals with
the abilities of ten or a
hundred men, there should be no
employment of them; I would make the
people, while looking on death as a
grievous thing, yet not remove
elsewhere (to avoid it).

Though they had boats and carriages,
they should have no occasion

to ride in them; though they had buff
coats and sharp weapons, they
should have no occasion to don or use
them.

I would make the people return to the
use of knotted cords (instead
of the written characters).

They should think their (coarse) food
sweet; their (plain) clothes
beautiful; their (poor) dwellings places
of rest; and their common
(simple) ways sources of enjoyment.

There should be a neighbouring state
within sight, and the voices
of the fowls and dogs should be heard
all the way from it to us, but I
would make the people to old age, even
to death, not have any
intercourse with it.

81

Sincere words are not fine; fine words
are not sincere. Those
who are skilled (in the Tao) do not
dispute (about it); the
disputatious are not skilled in it. Those
who know (the Tao) are not
extensively learned; the extensively
learned do not know it.

The sage does not accumulate (for
himself). The more that he
expends for others, the more does he
possess of his own; the more that
he gives to others, the more does he
have himself.

With all the sharpness of the Way of
Heaven, it injures not; with
all the doing in the way of the sage he
does not strive.